Disney

FROZEN

HAIRSTYLES

EDDA USA

DISNEY FROZEN HAIRSTYLES — Inspired by Anna & Elsa

© 2014 Disney Enterprises, Inc.

Author: Theodora Mjoll Skuladottir Jack
Photographer: Gassi.is
Photographer, p.32-35, 56-59 : Saga Sig, sagasig.com
Illustrations pages 4-9 © Aadarsh Pvt limited
Set designer: Rebekka A. Ingimundardottir
Stylist: Magnea Einarsdottir
Makeup artist: Sigurlaug Drofn Bjarnadottir
Layout and design: Elsa Nielsen, nielsen.is
Cover design: Gassi.is
Editors: Tinna Proppe, tinna@eddausa.com and Greta Bjorg Jakobsdottir
Printing: Printed in Slovenia

Second Edition

Distributed by Midpoint Book Sales & Distribution

ISBN: 978-1-94078-709-1

www.eddausa.com

WELCOME

... to the wonderful and breathtaking world of
Frozen. Join us in creating beautiful hairstyles
inspired by our favorite Disney sisters, Anna and Elsa.
In this book, you will find a variety of hairstyles
perfect for active girls and also for special occasions.
Each hairstyle is demonstrated with step by step
photographs and detailed instructions, to take
you on an exciting journey where you will find
something new and different to do with your hair.

Don't hesitate to jump right in and experiment, to combine
styles and create your own Frozen-inspired look.

Hop on the sled and enjoy the adventure with us!

Braidschool

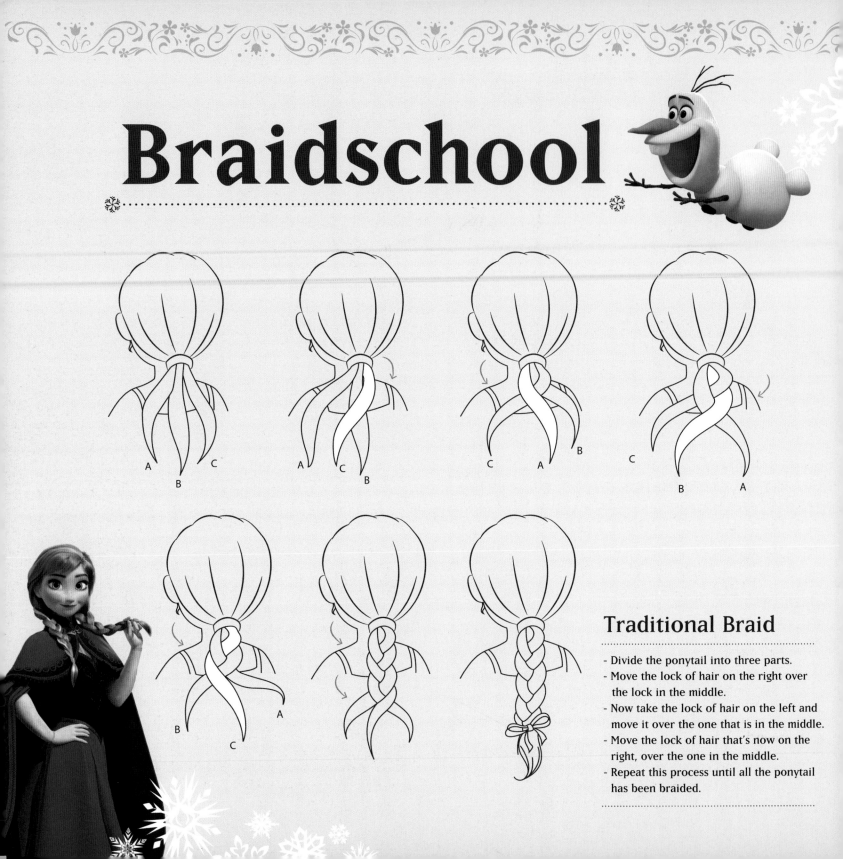

Traditional Braid

- Divide the ponytail into three parts.
- Move the lock of hair on the right over the lock in the middle.
- Now take the lock of hair on the left and move it over the one that is in the middle.
- Move the lock of hair that's now on the right, over the one in the middle.
- Repeat this process until all the ponytail has been braided.

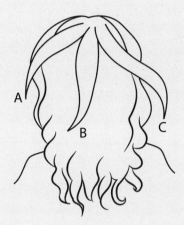
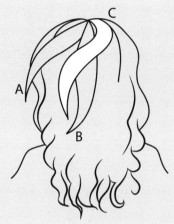
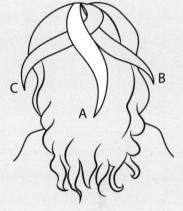

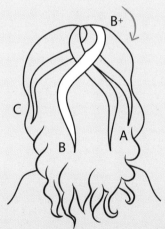

French Braid

- Take three locks of hair along the hairline in the front.
- Move the lock of hair on the right over the lock in the middle.
- Now take the lock of hair on the left and move it over the one that is in the middle.
- Take the lock of hair on the right and add a small lock of hair laying next to it, to the lock.

- Move the lock of hair on the right along with the added hair over the lock of hair in the middle.
- Repeat this process to the lock of hair on the left.
- Repeat this process all the way down or until all the hair on the head has been added to the braid.
- When all the hair has been added to the braid, make a traditional braid down the length of the hair.

Dutch Braid

- Take three locks of hair along the hairline in the front.
- Move the lock of hair on the right under the lock in the middle.
- Now take the lock of hair on the left and move it under the one that is in the middle.
- Take the lock of hair on the right and add a small lock of hair laying next to it, to the lock.

- Move the lock of hair on the right along with the added hair under the lock of hair in the middle.
- Repeat this process to the lock of hair on the left.
- Repeat this process all the way down or until all the hair on the head has been added to the braid.
- When all the hair has been added to the braid, make a traditional braid down the length of the hair.

Rope

- Divide the ponytail in two.
- Twist both locks in the same direction.
- When both locks have been twisted a little bit,
  cross them once in the opposite direction to the twist.
- Keep twisting the locks in the same direction as before
  and cross the locks in the opposite direction to the twist.
- Repeat the process down the length of the hair.

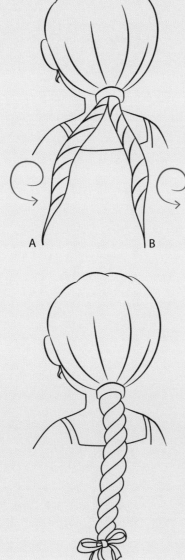

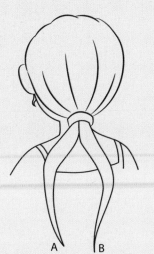
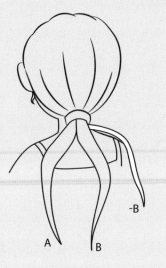
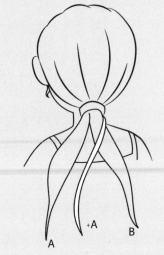
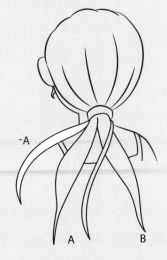

A   B   A   -B   A +A B   -A   A   B

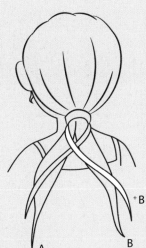
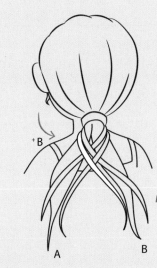
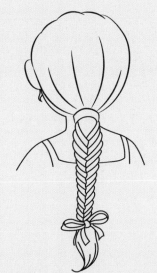

+B   A   B   +A   A   B   +B   A   B

Traditional Fishtail Braid

- Divide the ponytail in two.
- Take a small lock from the outside of the right half of the hair.
- Move the lock over the half of the hair and under the left half of the ponytail.
- Combine the lock with the hair on the left.

- Take an identical lock of hair from the outside of the left half of the hair and move it over to the right part.
- Combine the lock with the hair on the right.
- Repeat this process down the length of the hair.

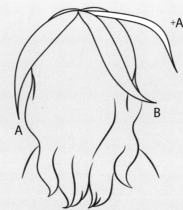
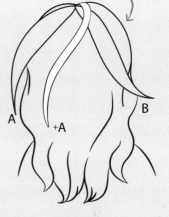

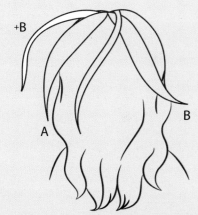
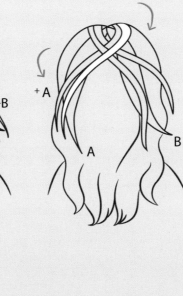

French Fishtail Braid

- Take two locks of hair along the hairline in the front.
- Take a small lock of hair from the head just beside the big lock on the right and move it over the big lock and combine it with the big lock of hair to the left.
- Now take a small lock of hair from the head just beside the big lock of hair on the left and move it over to the lock of hair on the right.

- Take another small lock of hair from the head beside the big lock on the right and move it over the lock of hair on the left.
- Repeat this process down the head until all the hair has been added to the braid.
- When all the hair has been added to the braid, continue on by braiding a traditional fishbraid down the length of the hair.

Twists and Braids

1.

2.

3.

4.

5.

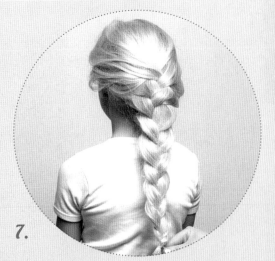

6.

Elsa's Icy Braid

1. Curl the hair with medium-sized curling tongs. It's best to start at the bottom and work your way to the top.
2. Lightly backcomb the hair at the top by the root.
3. Take hold of three fairly large locks of hair from the sides and start making a French braid (see the Braidschool, p. 5).
4. Add fairly large locks to the braid and keep it quite loose.
5. Continue making the braid down the length of the hair.
6. Pull the ends of the braid. It works well to hold onto the end of the braid with one hand while pulling its ends with the other hand.
7. Put a small elastic band at the end.

7.

13

 1.

 2.

 3.

4.

 5.

 6.

 7.

 8.

9.

10.

Braidless Braid

1. Take the top section of the hair and put it in a ponytail. Place a topsy tail™, a little hairstyling tool, underneath the ponytail, as shown in the picture.

2. Thread the hair from the ponytail through the loop and pull the topsy tail™ with the ponytail down the head.

3. Tighten the hair against the twist that forms by pulling the locks of the ponytail apart, but close to the elastic band.

4. Now take hold of an equally large lock of hair below the first one and put it in an elastic band. Place the elastic band below the first ponytail and add the hair from the first ponytail.

5. Place the topsy tail™ behind the elastic band in the same manner as before.

6. Pull the hair through and carefully tighten it against the twist that forms.

7. Repeat the process down the length of the head. When all the hair has been arranged in ponytails, place an elastic band around the ponytail an inch or two below the last one.

8. Open the hair in between the elastic bands and pull the hair through.

9. Now put an elastic band around the hair in the same manner as before, at an equal distance, then pull the hair through as before.

10. Repeat the process down the ponytail.

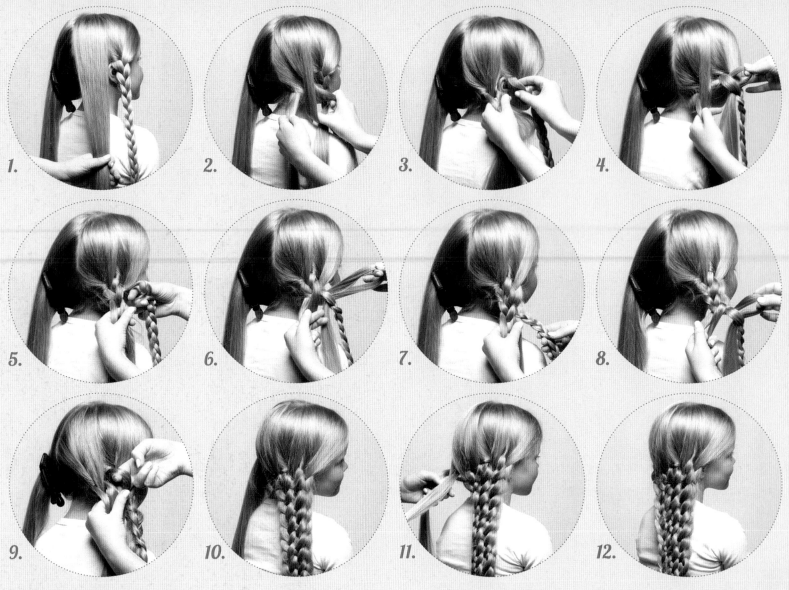

Big Braid

1. Divide the hair into four equally large sections. Make a traditional braid (see the Braidschool, p. 4) in the section closest to the front, and put an elastic band on the end. Take the section next to the braid, and clip the rest of the hair away.
2. Braid the section once.
3. Open the first lock of the braid already made, the lock closest to the new braid.
4. Pull one lock of the new braid through the lock.
5. Braid once. Now open the lock below the former.
6. Pull one lock through again, and braid once.
7. Repeat this down the braid, repeatedly. You are actually making a traditional braid, only hooking it to the braid next to it.
8. Once the whole length has been added to the braid, put an elastic band at the end. Take hold of the third section.
9. Open the first lock of the braid that is next to it, and repeat the process.
10. Join all the braids in one elastic band.
11. Now take the last section of hair and add it to the big braid in the same way as before.
12. Be brave pulling the big braid apart and in different directions if you would like to make it wider.

1.   2.   3.   4.

5.   6.   7.

Braids Within a Braid

8.

1. Divide the hair in two, horizontally across the top of the head. Clip the lower section away.
2. Make a braid from the hair on one side, heading back.
3. Braid similarly on the other side, and fasten the two braids together at the back of the head with an elastic band.
4. Take two large locks of hair from either side of the head and start making a French braid.
5. Also add a large lock from underneath the loose braids. Use it as the third part of the French braid (see the Braidschool, p. 5).
6. Make the braid large, and make sure to include all the hair.
7. Pull the sides of the braid, to increase volume.
8. So that the little braids are better visible within the large braid, you can pull them to the front of the big braid afterwards.

Double Fishbraid

1. Divide the hair in two, horizontally across the top. Gather the lower section in a high ponytail.
2. Divide the section on top in two, either making a middle or side part.
3. Make a fishtail braid in one section (see the Braidschool, p. 8), heading back.
4. Similarly, make a fishtail braid in the section on the other side.
5. When both fishtail braids are ready, make a hole above the ponytail.
6. Push the hair from the ponytail up and through the hole.
7. Tighten the ponytail firmly when all the hair is through.
8. Put the two braids through the hole in the ponytail.
9. Pin the hair together by the elastic band to conceal it.

9.

1.

2.

3.

4.

5. 6.

7. 8.

Twist and Turns

❄ .... ❄

9. 10.

1. Take hold of two large locks of hair on one side. Pin the rest of the hair away.
2. Make a rope from the locks and put an elastic band on the end.
3. Take two locks above the rope and create another rope (see the Braidschool, p. 7)
4. Make another rope behind the former two. Make sure that all the ropes twist in the same direction.
5. Now make the fourth rope on the other side of the head.

6. Put loose hair in a side ponytail at the back. Open one of the ropes where it meets the ponytail.
7. Put the ponytail through the hole in the rope.
8. Open all the ropes around the ponytail in the same manner.
9. Wrap the ropes once around the ponytail.
10. Put a transparent elastic band around the ends of the ropes and the ponytail.

Hidden Knots

❄ ⋯⋯⋯⋯⋯⋯⋯⋯⋯⋯⋯⋯⋯⋯⋯⋯⋯⋯⋯⋯⋯⋯⋯⋯⋯ ❄

1. Take two small locks on either side of the face and bring them to the back of the head.
2. Cross the locks over one another, as if you were making a little knot, and tighten them firmly.
3. Take locks below the first ones, and join them with the first locks.
4. Knot in the same manner as before.
5. Take another two locks below the former locks and join them. Make a knot.
6. Continue this down the length.
7. When all the hair has been gathered in knots, put an elastic band on the end.
8. Fold the end in behind the knots. Pin it down.
9. Fix the knots and use hairspray if you think it's needed.

9.

1.

2.

3.

4.

5.

Anna's Braids

1. Divide the hair in two sections. Make a shallow side part at the front. If you have a light hair lock or a ribbon, by all means fasten it in the hair on one side.
2. Bring all the hair on one side over the ear and divide it into three parts. Braid the hair, with the lock closest to the face added first into the braid.
3. Put a small elastic band on the end.
4. Take a small lock from below the elastic band and wrap it around it.
5. Pin the end down by placing a bobby pin behind the braid and pressing it. You can also use a small rubber band, which holds longer.

Braided Waterfall

1. Divide the hair in three parts, vertically down the head. Make the middle section a little smaller than the other two.
2. Clip each section so they remain separated.
3. Loosen the middle section. Take three small locks by the forehead and start making a Dutch braid (see the Braidschool, p. 6).
4. Make the braid a little to one side, braiding as firmly as you can.

5. Put an elastic band at the end, but note that it is unnecessary to braid all the way down the length.
6. Now take hold of the hair by the hairline on one side. Put the end of a topsy tail™, a little hairstyling tool (see picture), through a lock in the second round of the braid and thread the hair into the loop.
7. Pull the topsy tail™ with the hair through the lock.
8. Take another lock from the side, behind the

first one, and put the topsy tail™ through a lock of the braid, behind the former one. Pull the topsy tail™ with the hair through the lock.
9. Repeat the process down the head.
10. Take care to draw the hair all the way from the hairline into the braid. All the hair on one side should go through the braid.
11. When all the hair has come through, the hair style looks like this from the back.
12. It looks pretty to push the hair forward over the shoulder and hide the end of the braid in the length of the loose hair.

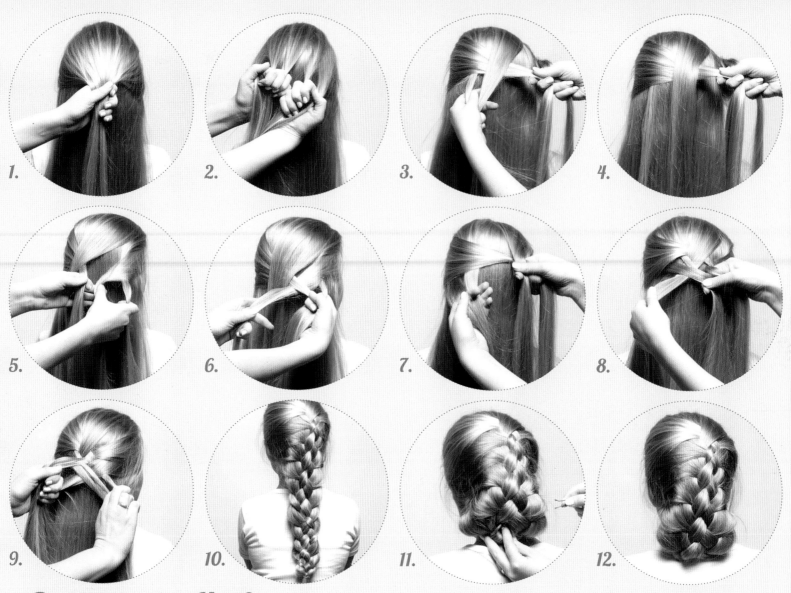

1.

2.

3.

4.

5.

6.

7.

8.

9.

10.

11.

12.

Braid and a Half

1. Take a fairly large lock of hair from the front and hold it at the back.
2. Divide it into five equal parts.
3. The simplest way is to look at the braid as two normal braids, i.e. concentrate on three parts at a time. Start braiding three locks on the right in one round.
4. When one round is finished, move over to the two locks that remain on the left side.
5. Braid them once with the lock of hair from the middle.
6. After braiding once, take hold of an extra lock, next to the lock furthest to the right, and join them.
7. Now move over to the left side again, and braid the three locks (closest to the right hand side) in the same manner as before. Add one lock to the lock furthest to the left in the same manner as on the other side.
8. Braid once with the new lock and then move over to the right side.
9. Take another lock of hair and join it with the lock furthest to the right. Braid once.
10. Continue in this manner down the head, or until all the hair has been gathered in the braid. Make a "normal" five-lock braid down the length and put an elastic band at the end.
11. Roll the hair under the braid and fasten it by pinning the hair together under the braid.
12. It isn't necessary to fasten the braid in this way, as it also looks beautiful hanging loose.

NOTE. This is the same braid as the five-lock braid from page 44, except here it is also a French braid. It works well to study the easier braid before tackling this one.

1.

2.

3.

4.

5.

6.

Winter Braid

❆ ⋯⋯⋯⋯⋯⋯⋯⋯⋯⋯⋯⋯⋯⋯⋯⋯⋯⋯ ❆

1. Comb all the hair back and take hold of three locks at the top by the forehead — two small locks and one large one.
2. Braid the locks in a Dutch braid (see the Braidschool, p. 6).
3. Add small amounts of hair to the small locks, but larger amounts to the large lock of the braid.
4. When the braid has started to take shape, pull the large lock out to the sides to form "wings".
5. Shape and pull the large lock on both sides.
6. Braid all the way down to the nape of the neck using the same method as before.
7. Place an elastic band on the end. Take a small lock from the ponytail and wrap it around the elastic band. Fasten the end down with a bobby pin.

7.

1.
2.
3.
4.

5.
6.
7.
8.

9.
10.
11.

Cross Braid

1. Divide the hair into four equal parts. Clip each part separately.
2. Loosen the top section on the right side.
3. Take three locks close to the ear and start making a French braid.
4. Only add hair from the top of the head into the braid, and direct it diagonally down the head.
5. When all the hair from this section has been added to the braid, loosen the bottom left section.
6. Continue braiding diagonally down the head, but add hair from the bottom section to the braid.
7. When all the hair from the bottom section has been added to the braid, place a small elastic band on the end.
8. Now loosen the top section on the left side.
9. Braid it towards the middle in the same manner as the section next to it.
10. Loosen the bottom right section, and bring the braid which is in the making, over the former braid.
11. Add hair from the bottom part to the braid in the same way as before. Place an elastic band on the end.

Updos and Buns

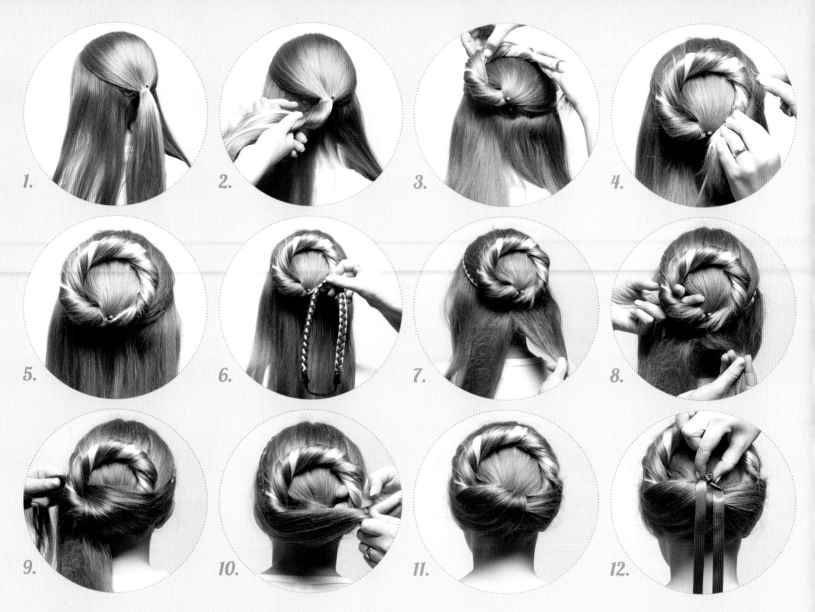

Anna's Crown

1. Pull aside hair by the hairline on either side and put the middle section in a low ponytail. Tie a ribbon around the ponytail.
2. Start twisting the hair from the ponytail tightly.
3. Twist the ponytail, up along the head in a circle.
4. Pin the bun tightly down around the circle.
5. Try to make the twist as even as possible throughout the circle.
6. Put a braided hairband around the hair. If the child has very thick hair, take a lock from underneath the twist, braid it and wrap it around the hair instead of the hairband.
7. Lightly backcomb the loose hair and divide it in two.
8. Take hold of the left section and put two fingers under the twist on the right side.
9. Pull the hair through, underneath the twist.
10. Do the same thing on the other side.
11. Press the ends of the hair into the bun that has formed at the back, and pin the hair down. It's best to hook the pin into the bulge and the root of the hair, then push it in and down into the hairdo.
12. Decorate the middle of the hairdo with hair accessories à la Anna.

Fit for a Queen

Note: This hairstyle works best if you curl the hair beforehand.

1. Divide the hair into two sections, horizontally across the top of the head. Put the lower section in a low ponytail and clip the top section away.
2. Twist the ponytail. Hold with one hand around the end of the twist and pull its sides with the fingers of the other hand.
3. Place the rolled up hair in a circle around the ponytail. Keep it quite loose.
4. Fasten the bun down by sliding bobby pins into the bun and against it. Keep the bun quite irregular, as it is prettier that way.
5. Loosen the top section once the bun has been fastened, and backcomb lightly at the root.
6. Divide the section in two.
7. Bring the right section over the left side of the bun, and pin it down (as in the picture).
8. Now bring the left section over the right side of the bun, and pin it down lightly. Take care

not to pull the hair tightly, as the style should remain casual.
9. Twist the ends a little and pull them around like you did with the ponytail (at the beginning).
10. Wrap the hair loosely around the bun, and fasten the end into the bun.
11. Do the same thing with the other loose lock.
12. Pull the hairstyle and fix it as you wish. Remember that it should look irregular so there is no need to be too precise.

Bun and Braid

1. Divide the hair in two, vertically across the top of the head. Place the bottom section in a ponytail directly at the back.
2. Put a hair donut (as seen in picture) around the ponytail and fasten it with 2-3 bobby pins.
3. Distribute the hair evenly over the donut and put a thin elastic band around it.
4. Bring the hair that came from the donut to either side of it. Divide the top part of the hair in two, and bring the section on the left over the right side of the bun.
5. Divide this section in two. Take another lock from the top layer of the hair that came from the donut. Braid these three locks once.
6. Take an equally thick lock of hair from below the first one, and add it to one lock of the braid. Braid once.
7. Repeat the process down the bun, or until approximately half of the loose hair has been added to the braid.
8. Wrap the braid around the bun, and pin the end down.
9. Now take the section from the right side and bring it over to the left side of the bun.
10. Braid the section together with the loose hair from the bun in the same way as before.
11. When all the hair has been added to the braid, wrap it around the bun, and fasten the end with a bobby pin.
12. Pull and fix the braids to your liking.

1.

2.

3.

4.

5.

6.

7.

8.

Five in One

9.

10.

11.

1. Divide the hair in two, horizontally across the top. Clip the lower section securely away from the other section.
2. Divide the top section into five equal parts.
3. It is easiest to treat the braid as two normal braids; to concentrate on three locks at a time. Start by braiding three locks on the right, one round.
4. When you have braided them once, move over

to the locks that were left behind on the left side. Braid them once with the middle lock.
5. Now move over to the right side again, and braid the three locks on the right once together in the same manner as before.
6. Here, you can see that a braid is starting to form.
7. Now, move over to the left side, and braid the three locks on the left side once together in the same way as before.

8. Tighten the braid firmly so that it does not come undone.
9. Continue this method down the length of the hair.
10. Put an elastic band at the end and pull the sides of the braid as you wish.
11. It's pretty to use a transparent elastic band, or an elastic band in the same color as the hair.

All up in Knots

1. Take hold of one-third of the hair on top of the head. Divide this hair into two equal parts.
2. Take the two parts and cross them over one another as if you were making a knot.
3. Tighten the knot firmly and make another knot after the first one.
4. Make knots in succession all the way down the hair and put an elastic band at the end. This makes a knotted ponytail.
5. Divide the rest of the hair in two and make knots in the middle section in the same manner as before.
6. Repeat the knotting process for the lowest section as well.
7. Take the end of the first knotted ponytail up to the first knot, and stick it through there. It works well to put a hand underneath the first ponytail and drag the end through with the fingers.
8. Take the bun that has formed and pin it securely with bobby pins. It's best to hook the pins into the knots and at the roots and press them in. This way, both the pins and the hairstyle stay in place.
9. Repeat this process with the other knotted ponytails.

9.

Braided Crown

1. Put all the hair into a high ponytail.
2. Place a hair donut (as seen in picture) around the ponytail and fasten it down with 2-3 bobby pins. It's best to hook the pin into the root of the hair and the donut, and then press it in.
3. Distribute the hair evenly over the donut and put a thin elastic band around it.
4. Pull the ends of the hair down along the sides of the head with the hair distributed evenly between the two sides.
5. Take hold of three small locks from the right of the bun, but stand on the left and pull the locks towards you.
6. Braid the locks once together. Take another small lock next to the others, and add to one of them. Braid once.
7. Now take another lock next to the former, and add it to a lock. Braid once.
8. Continue this method until half of the loose hair has been added to the braid. Then braid all the way down the length. Remember to pull the braid towards you while braiding.
9. Do the same thing on the other side of the bun. Move to the right of the bun, pull the left side of the hair towards you, and braid in the same manner as before.
10. Take the first braid and wrap its end around the bun. Fasten the end down with a bobby pin.
11. Now move the second braid around the bun and fasten its end with a bobby pin. Pull the braid and fix it from above as it can stick up nicely from the bun. Or- Pull the braid as you wish.

Blue Ribbon

1. Divide the hair in two, across the back of the head. Pin the upper part away and make a side ponytail in the lower part. Hook a blue ribbon into the elastic band.
2. Comb the whole upper part to one side and fix it with bobby pins along the head to keep the hair in place.
3. Start gradually rolling the hair by the hairline in the direction away from the face. Start at the front by the forehead.
4. Roll this whole section in the same way down the side of the head, firmly against the hairline.

5. Bring the rolled up hair underneath the ponytail.
6. Wrap it around the ponytail to form a bun. Pin the bun down.
7. Now twist the hair from the ponytail then wrap the ribbon around the twist.
8. Place the twist around the bun, in the same direction as the bun.
9. It works well to pin the twist down as you set it in place.
10. Pin the bun down until it is firm and fix the hair and the ribbon to your liking.
11. It's good to tuck the end into the bun to conceal it.

1. **2.** **3.** **4.**

5. **6.** **7.** **8.**

9. **10.**

Circled Braid

1. Comb all the hair forward. It works well if the child leans forward while the braiding takes place.
2. On one side, grasp some hair by the hairline.
3. Start making a Dutch braid (see the Braidschool, p. 6).
4. Draw the hair into the braid with your fingers, or with a comb, to keep the braid firmly on top of the head/close to the forehead.
5. Draw fairly large locks into the braid. They should be big.
6. Continue the braid horizontally across the head, from ear to ear.

7. When all the hair has been added to the braid, then make a normal braid down the length. Pull the sides of the braid as you wish. The more you pull, the more volume the braid will have.
8. Bring the end of the braid back to the hairline. Bend the end in under the braid to hide it.
9. Fasten the braid with bobby pins. It works well to hook the pins into the braid and the roots of the hair, then press them in against the braid.
10. The perfect Circle Braid!

Zik Zak Bun

1. and 2. Take aside a large lock of hair at the top and put the lower section in a ponytail at the back of the head.
3. Grasp the top lock and braid it towards the ponytail.
4. When the braid has reached the ponytail, take a small lock from the ponytail.
5. Braid one round, including the ponytail lock, then take another lock from the ponytail and add it to one part of the braid as before.
6. Repeat the process down the ponytail. Hold the braid to the side and draw the locks into the braid that way.
7. When all the hair from the ponytail has been added to the braid, tie a small elastic band at the end.
8. Lift under the braid at the top.
9. Draw the end of the braid through until about half of the ponytail is through.
10. Now pin the braid down. It's best to hook the braid into the root of the hair and press the pin into the hair.
11. Put the end of the ponytail/braid around the bun, which has formed and pin it down with bobby pins.
12. It works well to tuck the end of the ponytail/braid into the bun to hide it and fasten it with a bobby pin.

1.
2.
3.
4.
5.
6.
7.
8.
9.
10.
11.

Princess Crown

1. Create a circular part in the middle of the head.
2. Clip the hair carefully down around the middle section.
3. Take two locks at the top of the circle and cross them over each other.
4. When the locks have been crossed, take hair from either side of the locks, and add it. Cross the locks, including the extra hair, over one another.
5. Continue in this manner down the circle, and bend the twist in a circle along the part.
6. When half of a circle has been made, loosen the hair around the middle section.
7. Add hair from close to the ear to the twist, and continue adding hair to the twist in the same way as before.
8. Bring the twist close to the forehead.
9. Continue the twist down along the hairline.
10. When all the hair has been added to the twist, place it in a ponytail close to the roots of the hair.
11. Conceal the elastic band by taking a small lock from the ponytail, wrapping it around the elastic band and fastening it with a bobby pin.

1.

2.

3.

4.

5.

6.

Snow Queen

1. Gather all the hair in a ponytail at the back of the head.
2. Take one quarter of the hair and roll it up above the ponytail.
3. Fasten the hair with a bobby pin on both sides of the rolled up hair.
4. Now take one-third of the ponytail and roll it up next to it.
   Pin down the hair in the same way as before.
5. Repeat the process below the ponytail and on its other side.
   This creates a bun with four sections.
6. A flower or another hair decoration works nicely in the middle of the bun.

Waves and Ponytails

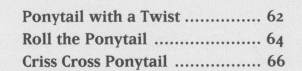

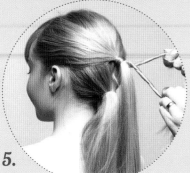
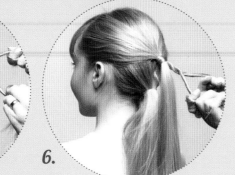

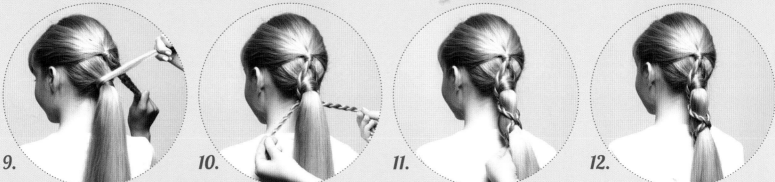

1.

2.

3.

4.

5.

6.

7.

8.

9.

10.

11.

12.

Ponytail with a Twist

1. Take aside fairly large locks of hair on either side at the front of the face and place the rest in a low ponytail.
2. Take the locks from the sides to the back of the head, and join them with a small elastic band. Take a small lock from the ponytail.
3. Wrap the small lock around the ponytail to conceal the elastic band and fasten it with a bobby pin underneath the elastic band.
4. Divide the ponytail in two parts.
5. Divide one of the parts in two again and twist both of its locks in the **SAME** direction (very important).
6. Entwine the twisted locks in the **OPPOSITE** direction of the twist of the locks. This creates a rope (see the Braidschool, p. 7).
7. Make a rope down the length and put a little elastic band at the end.
8. Do the same thing with the other part of the ponytail.
9. Now take a lock from the lower ponytail and twist it around the elastic band in the same way as with the upper ponytail.
10. Take the ropes and cross them under the lower ponytail.
11. Crisscross the ropes again over the ponytail and fasten them together underneath the ponytail by joining the ends with an elastic band.
12. It works well to include a small lock of hair from the lower ponytail in the elastic band so that the ropes stay secure in their places.

1.

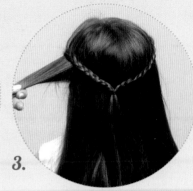
2.

3.

4.

5.

6.

7.

8.

Roll the Ponytail ❄ ⠤⠤⠤⠤⠤⠤⠤⠤⠤⠤⠤⠤⠤⠤⠤ ❄

1. Take hold of a fairly large lock of hair in the front by the face, and braid it down the length.
2. Make a similar braid on the other side, and fasten them together with a strong elastic band, directly at the back of the head.
3. Take hold of a fairly large lock below one of the braids.
4. Put two fingers under the braid and hook the lock of hair.
5. Pull the lock through. Now take another lock below the former, and join the two locks.
6. Put two fingers under the braid and hook the two locks.
7. Pull them through, towards the middle. Do the same thing on the other side.
8. Pull the hair over the braid so that it goes over the elastic band. It is optional how much hair is brought over the braid.
9. Pin the twist down by hooking the bobby pins into its sides and the roots of the hair. Then press them down and into the twist.

9.

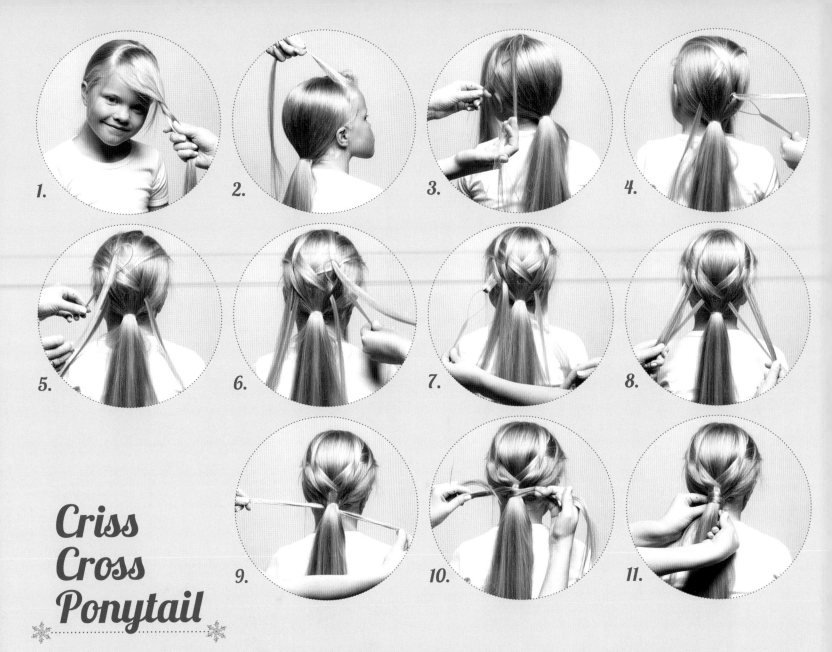

Criss Cross Ponytail

1. Take aside a fairly large lock of hair at the front of the face and place the rest of the hair in a low ponytail.
2. Grasp a small lock of hair on the right side.
3. Bring the lock back to the left side and put a topsy tail™ into the hair on the side. Thread the lock of hair through the loop and pull through.
4. Now take a small lock on the left and bring it over to the right side. Place the topsy tail™ in the same spot on the other side of the head, and draw the lock through.
5. Take a small lock next to the lock on the right side, and bring it over to the left. Place the topsy tail™ next to the earlier spot, a little closer to the ponytail.
6. Do the same thing on the other side.
7. Do this on alternate sides until all the hair is crisscrossing at the back.
8. Gather the locks of hair and pull them down to the ponytail.
9. Join the locks on either side and crisscross them under the ponytail.
10. Wrap them around the ponytail.
11. Pin the ends into and under the ponytail to hide them.

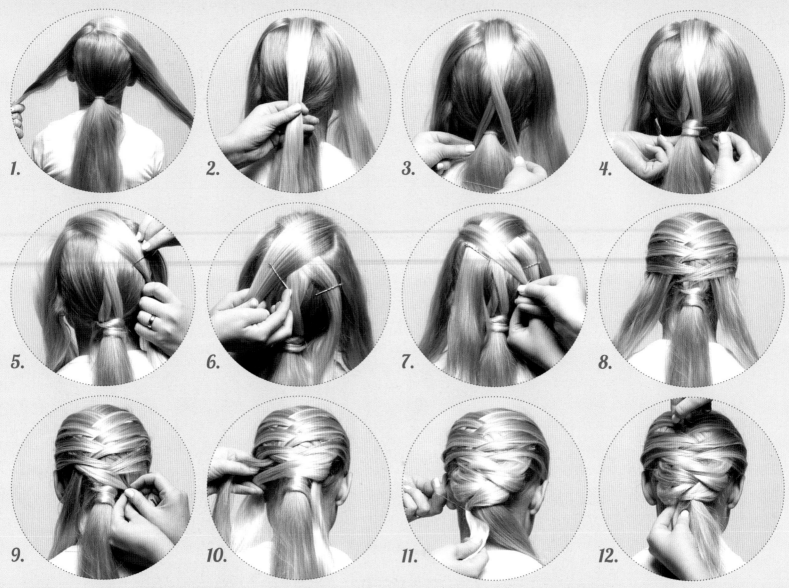

Frozen Wrap

1. Divide the hair in two, horizontally across the top of the head. Gather the bottom section in a low ponytail.
2. Take the hair in the middle of the top section back along the head.
3. Divide this lock in two and cross it over the ponytail.
4. Crisscross the hair repeatedly around the ponytail, until the elastic band is no longer visible. Pin the hair down. It's best to press the pin in and under the elastic band.
5. Take a lock from the left of the center and bring it over to the right side. Pin the lock down in the middle.
6. Take another lock, now from the right of the center, and bring it over to the left side. Pin it down in the same manner as before.
7. Now take a lock on the left side and bring it over to the right. Pin it down around the middle of the lock.
8. Take locks from the alternate side in this manner, or until all the hair from the front has been added to the hairdo at the back.
9. Divide the hair on one side in two, and bring it over the elastic band. Pin the hair down against the elastic band.
10. Do the same thing on the other side.
11. Gather the loose locks in an elastic band underneath the ponytail to hide them.
12. Remove the bobby pins that held the hairdo, but are now visible. No worries, the hairdo will not fall down.

Waves with Braids

1. Make a center part at the front. Take a lock next to the part on one side. Divide the lock in three and braid one round.
2. Now take a lock from the hairline.
3. Join the lock to one part of the braid.
4. Braid one round with the lock.
5. Take another lock by the hairline, below the first one.

6. Join the lock to one part of the braid as before, and braid one round.
7. Take a similar lock below the former and repeat the process.
8. Add approximately 2-3 similar locks to the braid and remember to add them from the hairline. Put an elastic band around the part when all the locks have been added to the braid.

9. Repeat the whole process on the other side of the head and join the two braids with an elastic band at the back of the head.
10. Take a lock from the ponytail and twist it.
11. Wrap the twist around the elastic band and pin down the ends of the twist with bobby pins.
12. Fix the twist and the braids to your liking.